Puzzle It!
Logic Puzzles and Tricks

by Dr. Moshe Levy

Designed & Illustrated
by Kathleen Bullock

Incentive Publications
Nashville, Tennessee

Cover by Angela Stiff
Edited by Marjorie Frank and Jill Norris
Copy edited by Cary Grayson and Stephanie McQuirk

ISBN 978-0-86530-517-5

Copyright ©2007 by Incentive Publications, Inc., Nashville, TN. All rights reserved. No part of this publication may be reproduced, stored in a retrieval system, or transmitted in any form or by any means (electronic, mechanical, photocopying, recording, or otherwise) without written permission from Incentive Publications, Inc., with the exception below.

Pages labeled with the statement ©**2007 by Incentive Publications, Inc., Nashville, TN** are intended for reproduction. Permission is hereby granted to the purchaser of one copy of **PUZZLE IT! LOGIC PUZZLES AND TRICKS** to reproduce these pages in sufficient quantities for meeting the purchaser's own classroom needs only.

1   2   3   4   5   6   7   8   9   10   10   09   08   07

PRINTED IN THE UNITED STATES OF AMERICA
www.incentivepublications.com

Contents

Welcome 5
How To Use 6

1. Mix & Match 7
2. Sock It to Me 7
3. Don't Miss the Boat 8
4. Relatively Puzzling 9
5. A Watery Dilemma 9
6. Let Them Eat Cake 10
7. To Tell the Truth 11
8. Liars & Truth-tellers 12
9. Conundrum on the Ice 13
10. Talking Turtles 14
11. The Pirate's Problem 15
12. The Queen's Necklace 16
13. Who Found the Mermaid? 17
14. Are You in Accord? 18
15. An Anniversary Toast 19
16. Fire on the Island 20
17. A Ringing Question 21
18. The Confused Professor 21
19. More Counterfeit Coins 22
20. Don't Lift That Pen! 23
21. Tricky Timekeeping 24
22. Another Timely Trick 24
23. Troublesome Ladies 25

24. A Wise Gardener	26
25. A Puzzling Match-up	27
26. To Be or Knot To Be?	27
27. Coffee with Milk, Please!	28
28. A Fork in the Road	29
29. The King's Gifts	30
30. The Great Egg-drop	31
31. Wonderful Wands	32
32. Some Fortress!	33
33. A Chocolate-Y Quandary	34
34. Sixteen Points	35
35. Positioning the Pillars	36
36. Family Crossings	37
37. Draw the Envelope	38
38. The Sugar in the Goblet	39
39. Pet Crossings	40
40. Who Owns the Aardvark?	41
41. The Ant and the Honey	42
42. How Wide Is the River?	43
43. An Oily Predicament	44
44. A Hair-splitting Query	45
45. Friends & Acquaintances	46
46. Hats Off to the Guests	47
47. The Mathematician's Wife	48
48. The Democratic Pirates	49
49. Pasha's Problem	50
50. A Colorful Mess	51
Answer Key	52

WELCOME
TO THE FUN OF LOGIC PUZZLES AND TRICKS

Everybody loves a puzzle! A puzzle is like an unsolved mystery, teasing you to be the one that unravels it. There are few things that match the feeling of satisfaction you experience when, after thinking long and hard about a puzzle, the solution suddenly materializes—clear as crystal. It is truly a magical moment, one that will be remembered.

This book contains some great puzzles to challenge your brain. You don't have to be an Einstein to figure them out; just use a little logic. And the helpful hint doesn't hurt, either!

Here's some more magic: When students wrestle with a puzzle, classroom learning is energized. Who can walk away from the invitation to tackle a puzzle? It's too much fun to try to figure it out. Even the most reluctant students seem to wake up and be drawn into the solution process. But puzzles are much more than fun! They give the brain a workout and nurture problem-solving skills.

Every classroom and home should offer many puzzle-solving opportunities. The critical thinking and problem-solving skills that are honed while solving puzzles are basic. They apply to every facet and subject area of learning. In solving puzzles, students make use of such thinking skills as logic, analysis, synthesis, sequencing, creativity, induction, and deduction—and they often must use several of these simultaneously! They must observe, ask questions, consider strategies, try different strategies, visualize different possibilities, and figure out why one thing works and another does not. Many puzzles also refine hand-eye or hand-mind coordination, spatial awareness, and mental gymnastics.

Puzzles must be a part of every serious curriculum. The puzzles in the **Puzzle It!** series challenge students to analyze information and use their critical thinking skills.

ABOUT THE PUZZLES IN THIS BOOK

These are primarily logic puzzles, although they make use of many other problem-solving skills as well. Some of the puzzles are just words, and require careful reading. Other puzzles require visualization of something—like a queen's necklace, a water container, or a line-up of turtles. Still others present a diagram or other graphic dilemma to solve. The puzzles are challenging. (Some of them are very challenging!) However, the solutions do not require complex or formal knowledge of mathematics. A young student just might be on an equal footing with a math professor when tackling many of them. There is no age limitation. They're ready to solve—for anyone who enjoys a mental challenge.

How to Use the Puzzles

- Look over a puzzle carefully. Read the instructions a few times.

- Consider the puzzle thoughtfully. Make sure the purpose of the puzzle is clear to you.

- Evaluate what to figure out.

- Experiment with different strategies and ideas. Try out different solutions.

- Take one puzzle at a time. A puzzle will grab you and won't let go until you figure it out. So let it swirl around in your head—even over a few days. Stay with it until you reach a solution.

- Try not to peek at the answers. Each of these puzzles has a hint. This should help you move toward a solution.

- You can tackle a puzzle alone, or share a puzzle with friends and tackle it together. Share ideas, discuss, argue—until you arrive at a solution.

- When you find a solution, discuss it with someone else. Explain the steps and strategies you used to reach your answer. Compare your solution and methods with someone else's.

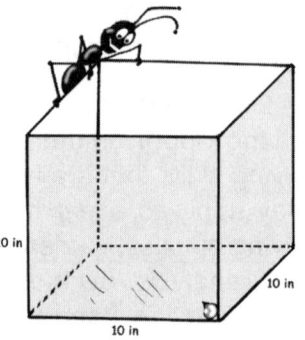

About the Solutions . . .

A logical solution is given for each of these logic problems. In some of the cases, however, there may be more than one solution that makes sense. Give credit for any solution that the puzzle-solver can explain logically.

What's the Source of These Puzzles?

Like the origin of many good jokes, folk tales, stories, or superstitions . . . the origins of many puzzles are hard to pinpoint. Puzzles such as those in this book are passed verbally from one person to another over generations. I am in debt to all those individuals who collected and distributed puzzles over the years (people such as Henry Dudeney, Sam Lloyd, Kendall and Thomas, Martin Gardner, Ruma Falk, and Ami Birenboim). They have inspired the inclusion of many puzzles in this book. I hope that you will join the puzzle-solvers and pass along the ones you like.

– Moshe Levy

Puzzle 1: MIX + MATCH

I have six identical matches. How can I use them to form four triangles without crossing or breaking any matches? Give it a try. Explain your solution.

Hint: page 63
Answer: page 52

Puzzle 2: SOCK IT TO ME

Max enters his room to get a pair of socks, but he doesn't want to turn on the light because his brother is sleeping. He knows that he has 12 white socks and 18 black socks in the drawer, but they are all mixed up. What is the minimum number of socks that Max needs to grab in order to ensure that he will have at least one pair of same-color socks?

Hint: page 63
Answer: page 52

Name_____

Puzzle It! Logic Puzzles and Tricks
©2007 by Incentive Publications, Inc., Nashville, TN.

Puzzle 3: Don't Miss the Boat!

Lucy washed up on a deserted island after her sailboat sank. Fortunately, she had a waterproof package holding a few matches, two pieces of rope, and one flare. Everything else went down with the boat, even her watch.

She knows that the Coast Guard patrols the area exactly one and a half hours after sundown. She also knows that each piece of rope will burn for exactly one hour. The problem is that the ropes are not uniform in thickness, so the speed at which a rope burns is not constant. (Half a rope does not necessarily burn in half an hour.)

How can she measure one and a half hours by burning the ropes so she will know exactly when to set off her flare? (If she sets off the flare at the wrong time, she'll miss her chance to notify the Coast Guard and get rescued.)

Hint: page 63
Answer: page 52

Puzzle 4 — RELATIVELY PUZZLING

Todd and Rob were born to the same mother on the exact same day (same year) in the same hospital. Yet, they are not twins. How is this possible?

Hint: page 63
Answer: page 52

Puzzle 5 — A WATERY DILEMMA

Nurse Terry needs exactly six quarts of water to refill the cooler down the hall. (The cooler is not portable, so she can't carry it to the sink for filling.) She is a bit inconvenienced because she does not have a 1-quart container or a 6-quart container. She has only a 4-quart container and a 9-quart container. How can she measure exactly six quarts with the containers she has?

Hint: page 63

Answer: page 52

Name_____

Puzzle It! Logic Puzzles and Tricks 9 ©2007 by Incentive Publications, Inc., Nashville, TN.

Puzzle 6: Let Them Eat Cake

I invited seven friends to my birthday party. I want to make only three straight cuts in this cake. How can I get eight pieces of equal size and shape?

Hint: page 63
Answer: page 52

Draw your answer:

Puzzle 7: To Tell The Truth

Which sentence(s) are true?

1. This note contains one false sentence.
2. This note contains two false sentences.
3. This note contains three false sentences.
4. This note contains four false sentences.
5. This note contains five false sentences.
6. This note contains six false sentences.
7. This note contains seven false sentences.
8. This note contains eight false sentences.
9. This note contains nine false sentences.
10. This note contains ten false sentences.
11. This note contains eleven false sentences.
12. This note contains twelve false sentences.
13. This note contains thirteen false sentences.
14. This note contains fourteen false sentences.
15. This note contains fifteen false sentences.
16. This note contains sixteen false sentences.
17. This note contains seventeen false sentences.

Hint: page 63
Answer: page 52

Puzzle 8: Liars + Truth-tellers

Astronaut Commander Juan DerLustt has landed on an unexplored planet with two types of inhabitants: liars and truth-tellers. The liars always lie and the truth-tellers always tell the truth.

The planet has two settlements. All the liars live in one settlement, and all the truth-tellers live in the other. The inhabitants trade with each other and routinely visit the neighboring settlement.

Commander DerLustt has arrived at one of the settlements and is trying to figure out if it is home to the liars or the truth-tellers. He has come across one of the aliens. What single question could the astronaut ask the alien that would tell which settlement he (the astronaut) is in?

This ought to be fun!

Hint: page 63
Answer: page 53

Conundrum on the Ice

Coach has given us this challenge to do on our break from practice: Arrange nine hockey pucks on the ice in such a way that ten straight lines could be drawn—each one passing through at least three dots. Show us how to do it.
Help!

Draw your answer here:

Hint: page 63
Answer: page 53

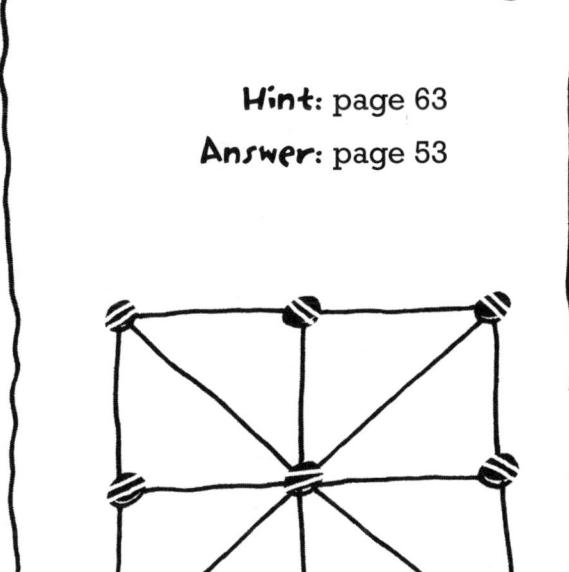

Name_____

Puzzle It! Logic Puzzles and Tricks 13 ©2007 by Incentive Publications, Inc., Nashville, TN.

Talking Turtles

Three turtles (unusual turtles—in that they can talk) are crawling along in the desert. As they move, they make some observations. Is it possible that they are all telling the truth?

The first turtle says: *In front of me I see the beautiful desert, and behind me I see two turtles.*

The second turtle says: *In front of me I see a turtle, and behind me I see a turtle.*

The third turtle says: *In front of me I see the beautiful desert, and behind me I see two turtles.*

Say, what's going on?
Hint: page 63
Answer: page 53

If so, how?

Puzzle 11: THE PIRATE'S PROBLEM

Pirate Jack Crusty hides out on the island of Wykiki. He needs to send a trunk of treasure to his friend, Pirate Fearsome Fran, who lives on the neighboring island of Wykookoo. Before his enemies track the treasure down and steal it from him, Jack needs to get it to Fran for safekeeping.

He wants her to remove the treasure from the trunk and hide it in some other container. One of Jack's ships can transfer the trunk between the two islands. The problem is that Jack is dreadfully sick and cannot possibly travel over the rough waters to Wykookoo. In addition, Fran has a fear of ships (an unfortunate ailment for a pirate), so she cannot make the trip either. Without Jack or Fran watching, the trunk might be opened and the treasure stolen, so Jack cannot transport the unaccompanied trunk unlocked.

Hint: page 63
Answer: page 53

Jack has a lock that can be put on the trunk, but that is of little help since the key is chained to his kitchen table; so, although the lock can be put on the trunk, the key can't be sent to Fran. She also has a lock, but her key is chained to her kitchen table. (Fran's key will not open Jack's lock, and Jack's key will not open Fran's lock.)

How can the treasure be safely shipped to Fran?

Propose your plan:

Name

Puzzle 12: The Queen's Necklace

The penny-pinching queen has five short golden chains, each made with four links. She wants one long necklace from all these chains, so she summons the Royal Goldsmith to ask him how much it will cost to create it. He tells her that it will cost $10 to open each link and weld it back together.

Ever so persnickety about money, the queen states: "What a lot of money for such a little job. This simple task will cost $50!"

The goldsmith replies, "No, actually, I can do it for less!"

If the goldsmith holds to his original quote ($10 for each link), how can he do the job for less?

Hint: page 63
Answer: page 53

It's tough being cheap and vain at the same time.

Puzzle 13: Who Found the Mermaid?

Four scuba divers explored four different locations. Each one came home with a favorite underwater photograph that captured part of his or her adventure. Which diver encountered a mermaid?

Mary did not dive anywhere in the Pacific Ocean.

The person who dove in Hawaii did not photograph a mermaid.

Larry did not photograph a sunken ship.

Harry did not dive in Belize.

A mermaid was not encountered in Bermuda or photographed in Belize..

The treasure chest was not photographed in Bermuda or Hawaii.

Terry did not dive in Australia.

Mary has never been to Bermuda.

A sunken ship was not photographed in Belize.

A lobster was photographed in the Northern Pacific Ocean.

Terry did not dive in Hawaii.

Harry did not photograph a treasure chest.

Hint: page 63
Answer: page 53

Puzzle 14 — ARE YOU IN ACCORD?

The Accord Apartment house has five floors. The elevator door on each floor is painted a different color. Tenants who live on each floor share a common interest; they meet regularly to discuss their interest, enjoy a specific snack at the meeting, and have a floor mascot.

None of the floors has the same color elevator door, meets on the same meeting night, serves the same snack, or has the same mascot.

One floor's mascot is a clown fish. The question is—which floor?

Hint: page 63
Answer: page 54

Clues:

- The floor that has Monday meetings has a red elevator door.
- The floor with regular Tuesday meetings has chosen a pug as its mascot.
- Twinkies are always served at the Wednesday discussion meetings.
- The green elevator door is on the floor above the white elevator door.
- After their meetings, some residents wipe the pizza sauce off their fingers so that it doesn't stain their white elevator door.
- Residents with the green elevator door always serve chips and salsa at their discussion meetings.
- The booklovers chose an owl as their mascot.
- The fast car buffs live on the floor with the yellow elevator door.
- The third floor always serves pizza rolls at discussion meetings.

- First floor discussion meetings are held on Thursday.
- The floor next to the physical fitness proponents has a Siamese cat mascot.
- The floor with a potbelly pig mascot is next to the floor of the fast car buffs.
- The current events floor is not next to the floor where residents enjoy cookies at the weekly discussion group.
- The antique collectors chose Friday for weekly discussion meetings.
- The floor with Thursday discussion meetings is next to the floor with the blue elevator door.
- Residents who eat cookies carry their books up the stairs to burn the extra calories they consume.
- The pug wears a green collar to match the elevator door on the floor where it lives.
- One health-conscious floor has fresh fruit at weekly discussion meetings.

Name_____

Puzzle It! Logic Puzzles and Tricks   18   ©2007 by Incentive Publications, Inc., Nashville, TN.

Puzzle 15: An Anniversary Toast

Zelda and Mortimer Whittier decided to toast each other with prune juice to celebrate their 50th anniversary. They had eight ounces of prune juice, which they decided to divide equally between the two of them. The prune juice was in an 8-ounce container, filled to the rim. To their dismay, they found that they did not have two glasses of the exact same size. They had only a 5-ounce glass and a 3-ounce glass. How could they divide the prune juice so they could be sure that each one would get exactly 4 ounces?

Hint: page 63

Answer: page 55

Puzzle 16

Fire on the Island

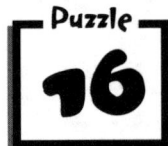

A shepherd is tending a herd of sheep on Baabaa Island. Suddenly, a raging fire starts on the north end of the small island. The fire spreads steadily southward with the wind, burning everything in its path. The shepherd has no way to extinguish a fire. He does not have a boat.

The sheep can't swim, nor can they jump over the fire. The good news is that the fire is moving very slowly, so the shepherd can run faster than the speed at which the fire is advancing. How can the shepherd save the sheep?

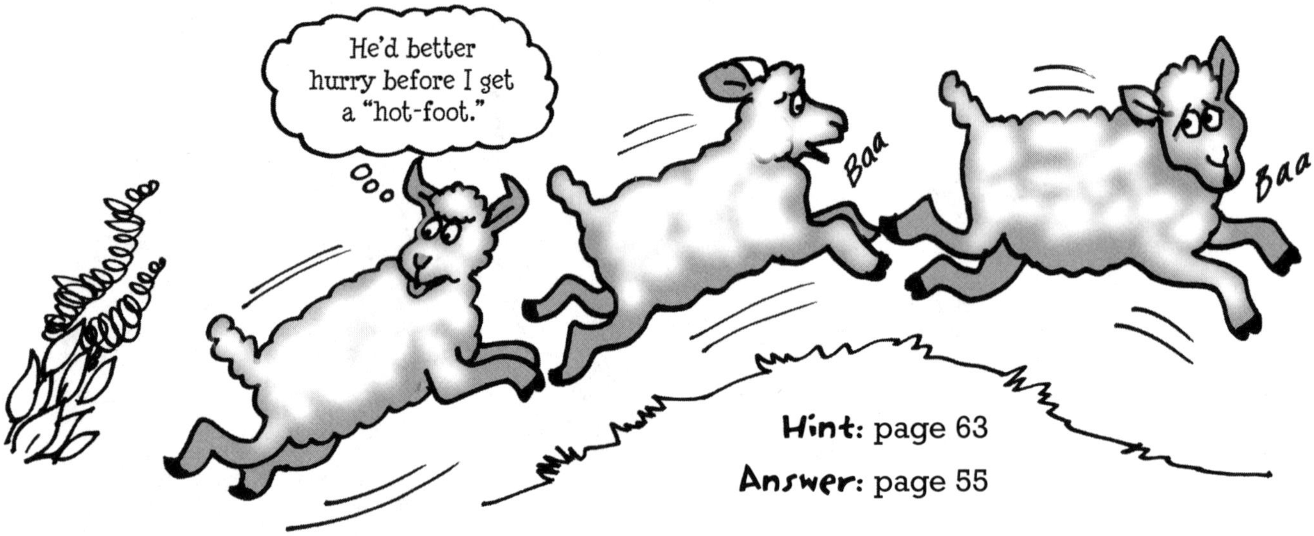
He'd better hurry before I get a "hot-foot."
Baa
Baa

Hint: page 63

Answer: page 55

Name____

Puzzle 17 — A Ringing Question

Hint: page 63
Answer: page 55

The bell tower at the university rings every hour to tell the time. It takes six seconds for the bell to ring six times. How long does it take the bell to ring eleven times?

Puzzle 18 — The Confused Professor

Hint: page 63
Answer: page 55

Logics professor Dr. Gustavas Axiom was in the bell tower at the university doing some research about the physics of the bell's sounds when he toppled to the ground. The fall gave him a slight concussion, leaving him confused. In this confused state, he sat down to write ten letters to his colleagues inviting each of them to a conference on logic. After he sealed the envelopes and started to write the names and mailing addresses, he realized that he had no idea which letter was in which envelope. He decided to write the names on the envelopes randomly.

What are the chances that exactly nine of the letters have the right name on the envelope (the same name as on the inside letter)?

Name_____

Puzzle It! Logic Puzzles and Tricks

Puzzle 19

COUNTERFEIT COINS

A robber creeps away from the bank with eight bags, each containing 100 coins. Unbeknownst to him, seven of the bags contain valuable gold coins, but the other bag contains counterfeit coins. When he hears the news report about the theft, he is astonished to learn that some of the coins are counterfeit, and he is anxious to find out which bag has the fakes.

He learns some other information from the news report: The counterfeit coins look exactly like the gold coins, but they weigh less. Each gold coin weighs 10 grams, and each counterfeit coin weighs only 9 grams.

The robber has time for one weight check on an electronic scale. How can he find out which bag contains the counterfeit coins with only one weighing?

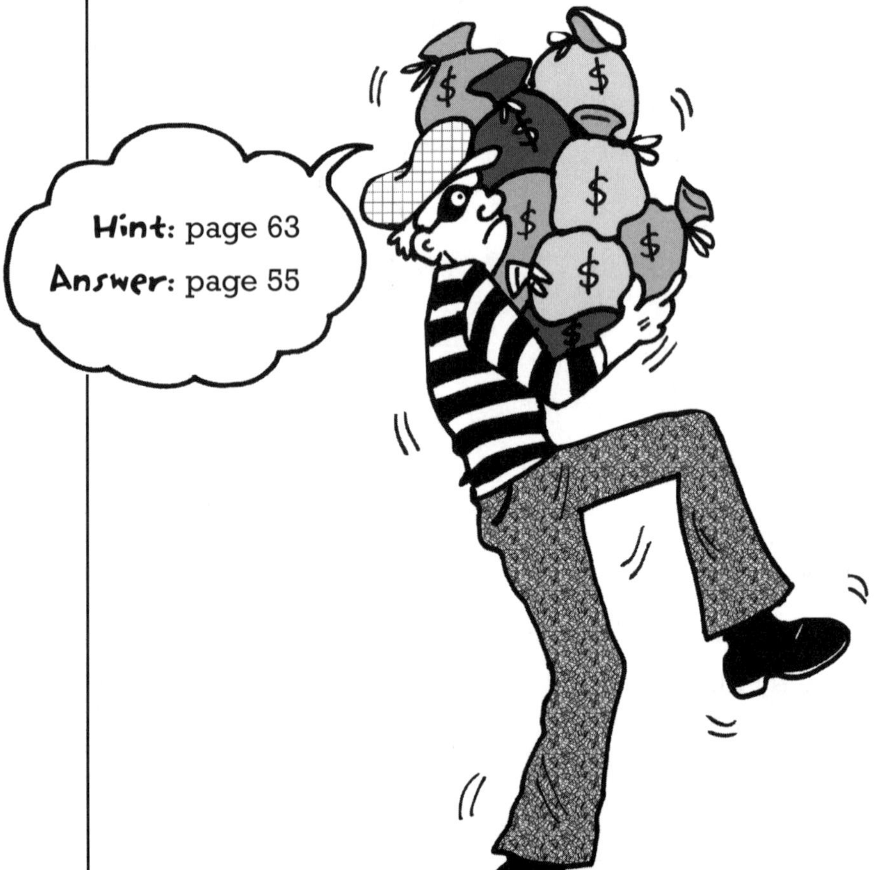
Hint: page 63
Answer: page 55

Name____

Don't Lift That Pen!

Without lifting your pen from the paper, connect the nine dots with four straight lines.

Hint: page 64
Answer: page 56

Puzzle 21 — Tricky Timekeeping

Miss Bee T. Imely is a creator of beautiful custom-made hourglasses. She makes each one to measure a precise time. Today, however, she is in a quandary. She finds that she MUST measure exactly nine minutes. She just sold her last 9-minute hourglass and has not had time to make any more. How can she use a 4-minute hourglass with a 7-minute hourglass to measure precisely nine minutes?

Hint: page 64
Answer: page 56

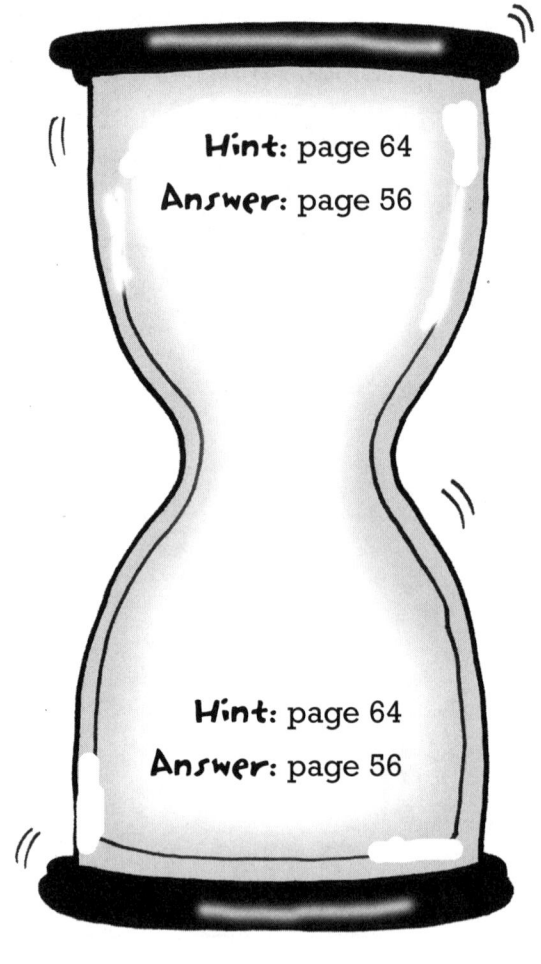

Hint: page 64
Answer: page 56

Puzzle 22 — Another Timely Trick

Hourglass-maker Bee T. Imely has two hourglasses with her in her car. One is an 11-minute hourglass. The other is a 7-minute hourglass. She is delivering them to a very distinguished customer. Bee arrives at the customer's gate. She has been instructed to ring the buzzer at the gate at precisely 3:17 pm. Although she has no watch or clock in the car, she knows that it must be before 3 pm because she left home at 2:15 pm for the 5-minute drive. She knows that the church chimes will begin ringing at exactly 3:00 pm. How can she use the hourglasses to measure exactly 17 minutes so she can ring the buzzer on time?

Puzzle 23: Troublesome Ladies

What a quarrelsome collection! These nine ladybugs just cannot get along with each other. Add two square fences to the pen to be sure that each of the ladybugs has her own separate compartment.

Hint: page 64
Answer: page 57

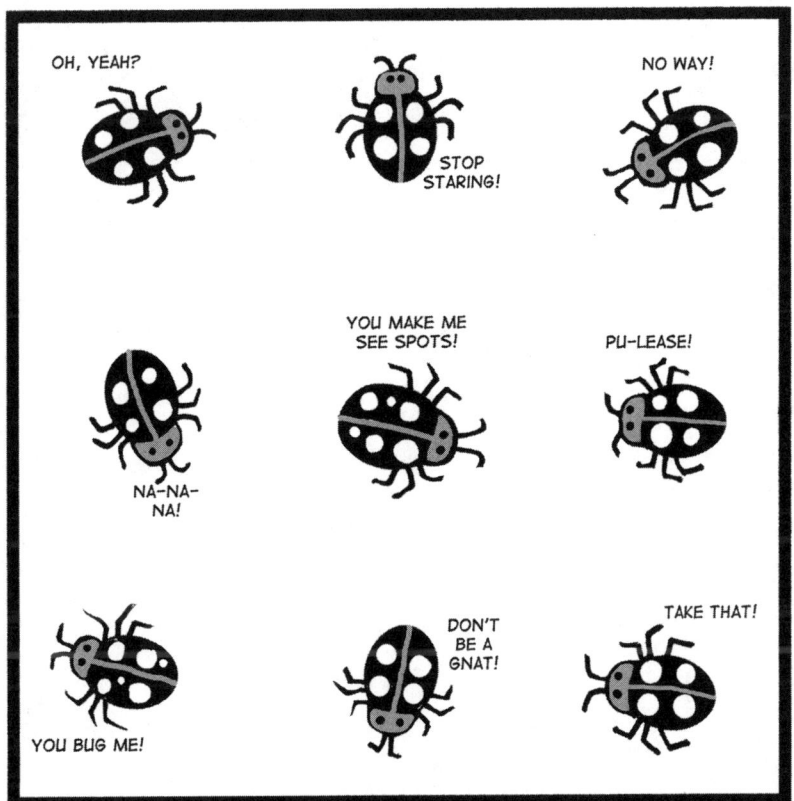

A WISE GARDENER

Wise King Solomon liked to surround himself with wise workers. So when he needed a gardener for his palace grounds, he looked for a smart one. He gathered all the applicants for the job together and gave them this challenge:

"I want to plant ten trees in the garden so that they form five straight lines with four trees in each line. The first of you to tell me how this can be done will get the job as the Royal Gardener."

Find one answer that will help someone get the job.

Hint: page 64

Answer: page 57

Name

Puzzle 25: A Puzzling Match-Up

Arrange eight matches so that they form four triangles and two squares. (Do not break or cross any of the matches.)

Hint: page 64
Answer: page 57

Puzzle 26: To Be or Knot To Be?

Try this trick! Take a simple piece of string at least 24" long and lay it on a table in front of you. The string should be in a straight line.
Pick up each end of the string with one hand, and without letting go, form a knot in the string. When you figure out how to do this, explain your method!

Hint: page 64
Answer: page 57

Puzzle 27 — Coffee with Milk, Please!

Hint: page 64
Answer: page 57

This cup of java is just right.

Ms. Geraldine Java, owner of the "Bean There" Coffee Shop, is mixing up a special new coffee-milk drink. She has a container with one gallon of coffee and a container with one gallon of milk. (Each of these containers is not full, but has more room besides what is taken up by the one gallon of liquid.)

She takes a 10-ounce cup, fills it to the rim with coffee from the coffee container, and pours it into the milk container. She mixes the milk with the coffee, then fills the cup to the rim from the milk container. (This milk now contains some coffee.) Then she pours this mixture back into the coffee container.

After this, is there more milk in the coffee container or more coffee in the milk container?

Puzzle 28 — A Fork in the Road

Alexander is vacationing on an unfamiliar island in a country far away from his home. He is looking for the beach when he comes to a fork in the road. The clerk at the hotel had warned Alexander about the fork and told him that one road would take him to the beach, while the other would lead him into a mosquito-infested swamp.

Unfortunately, Alexander didn't pay attention well, and he cannot remember which road is which. Just as he thinks he will have to head back to the hotel, a local resident happens along. This girl knows the way to the beach. But there is a problem: The island is inhabited by truth-tellers and liars. Truth-tellers always tell the truth. Liars always lie.

Alexander does not know whether this girl is a truth-teller or a liar. What is the one question Alex can ask to find out which road leads to the beach?

Trust me. The beach is that way.

Hint: page 64
Answer: page 58

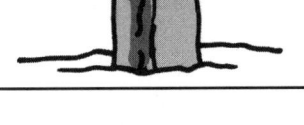

Puzzle 29

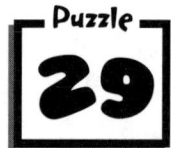

The King's Gifts

King Solomon wanted to send some gifts to three neighboring kings. He had his servants prepare three crates: one with gold coins, one with silver coins, and one with a mixture of both gold and silver coins. The crates were sealed, and signs were attached to each crate indicating its contents.

Ahhh, but as often happens with these things, there was a mix-up. Somebody placed all three signs incorrectly. Now, King Solomon must call upon his own wisdom to figure out the contents of all three crates. How can he do this by opening only one crate, and by looking at only a single coin from that crate?

Hint: page 64
Answer: page 58

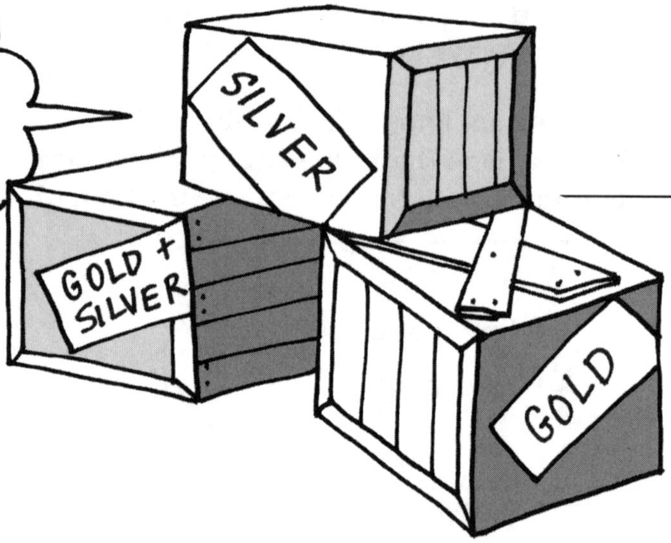

Name____________________

THE GREAT EGG-DROP

Dr. I. C. Proofs (the renowned physicist) hosted an Easter egg hunt for his 15 grandchildren. At the end of the day, he gathered up a basketful of leftover eggs. Still in a mischievous holiday mood, the scientist couldn't resist the urge to use the colorful eggs for an experiment.

Dr. Proofs thought about sending those brightly colored eggs sailing out some of the windows in the new 100-story building near the university. So, still wearing his Easter bunny suit, he set out to answer this question: "What is the highest floor in this building from which an egg can be dropped without the shell being smashed?"

He took his basket of eggs and ascended to different floors. What is the smallest number of eggs that Professor Proofs will need to smash on the grassy lawn outside the building in order to get a full and exact answer to his question?

Hint: page 64
Answer: page 58

Puzzle 31 — WONDERFUL WANDS

I can move three of these wands and **Presto -** I will form three squares instead of four. Can you?

Hint: page 64

Answer: page 58

SOME FORTRESS!

King Solomon asked his advisers to make a plan for ten new castles for the kingdom. He asked that the castles be built on five straight defense walls, such that there are four castles on each wall. His advisers came up with the following plan:

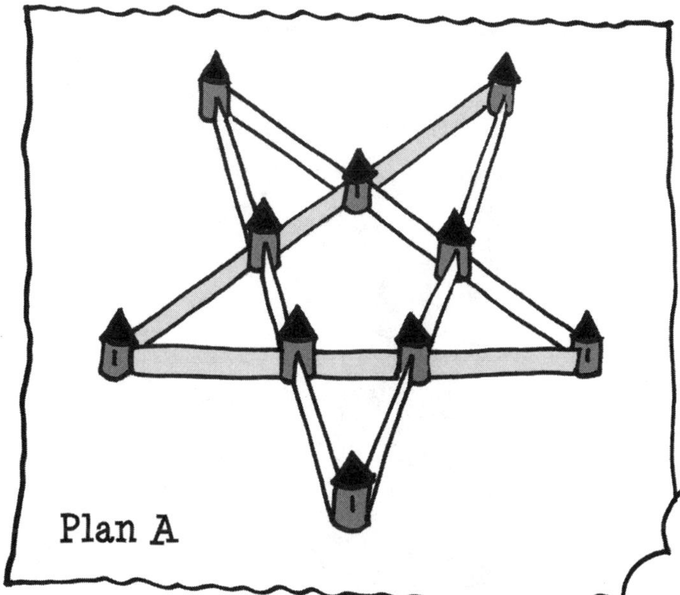

Plan A

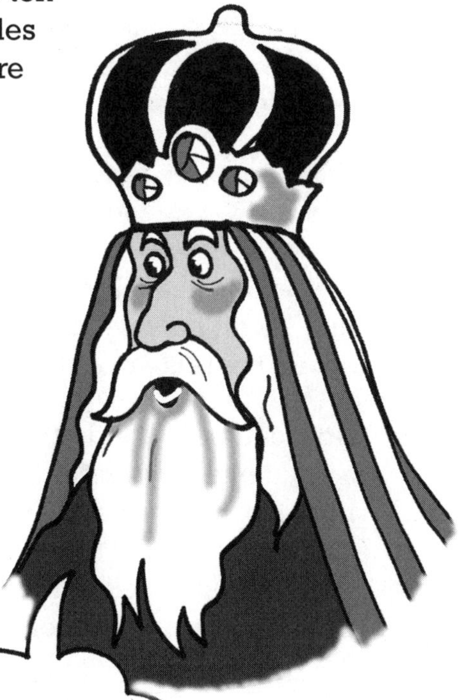

Hint: page 64
Answer: page 58

The king rejected this first plan. The problem, he said, was that every one of the castles was exposed to attack from the outside. He wanted the plan changed to form an arrangement that would keep at least two of the castles surrounded by walls from all sides. How can this be achieved? Draw your ideas here.

Puzzle 33: A Chocolate-y Quandary

The McKinley family reunion starts tomorrow. In all, 183 people will gather for a huge picnic to kick off the event. Three sisters, Sara, Sue, and Sandy, are in charge of getting the chocolate syrup for the ice cream dessert, and barrels for a relay.

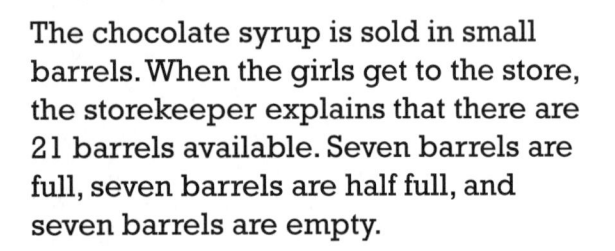

The chocolate syrup is sold in small barrels. When the girls get to the store, the storekeeper explains that there are 21 barrels available. Seven barrels are full, seven barrels are half full, and seven barrels are empty.

How can they divide the barrels so that each sister carries seven barrels, and they all have the same amount of syrup? (They want to do this without transferring any syrup from one barrel to another.)

> Figuring the amount of chocolate in each barrel was tricky, but worth it. Mmmm, yummy!

Hint: page 64
Answer: page 58

Sixteen Points

Can you draw six straight lines through the 16 points below without lifting your pen from the paper?

Puzzle 35: POSITIONING THE PILLARS

An ambitious architect decided to build a pavilion on 16 pillars. The pillars must be arranged in 15 straight lines of 4 pillars each.

How shall he design the pavilion to make this possible?

Some of the best brains in the country have worked on this project.

Hint: page 64
Answer: page 59

Try your ideas here.

Name _____

Puzzle It! Logic Puzzles and Tricks

Puzzle 36
FAMILY CROSSINGS

A family of two parents and two children needs to cross a river. They have a small kayak, which can carry only one adult, or two children. How can they cross?

Hint: page 64
Answer: page 59

Puzzle 37: Draw the Envelope

"I just drew this envelope without once lifting my pencil from the paper, and without drawing over any line twice. Can you do this?"

Hint: page 64
Answer: page 59

Puzzle 38: The Sugar in the Goblet

Charlie is having a great time fooling around with the utensils on the dinner table. He has arranged four knives to form a make-believe goblet, complete with a sugar cube inside.

How can he move only two knives to form an identical goblet, but this time with the sugar cube on the outside?

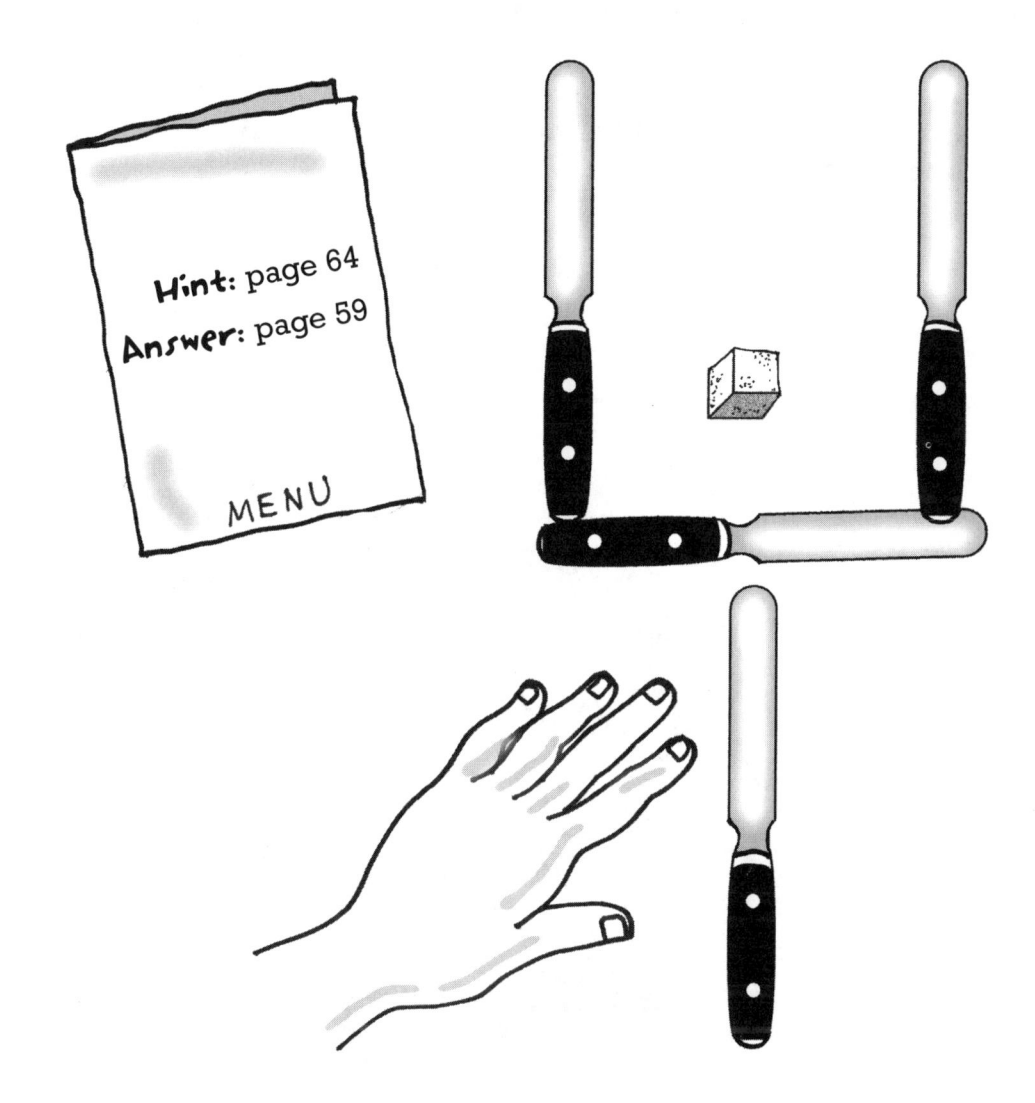

Hint: page 64
Answer: page 59

Puzzle 39: Pet Crossings

Agatha Abernathy takes at least one of her three pets everywhere she goes. Today, she needs to get all of them to the other side of the bridge to visit the veterinarian. Her dog, cat, and pet mouse all have appointments. The problem is that the basket on her bike is big enough for only one pet at a time.

None of the pets can walk along the bridge, because the traffic makes it a dangerous place for animals. The dog and cat cannot be left alone at any time, because the dog is sure to terrorize the cat (or worse). The cat and the mouse cannot be left alone together, even for a few seconds, because the cat will eat the mouse. The dog and mouse get along just fine. How can Agatha safely get all her pets across the bridge?

I have a fat cat, a fat rat, and a fat dog. Only one pet fits in my basket at a time.

Hint: page 64
Answer: page 59

Puzzle 40: Who Owns the Aardvark?

Five friends live in a row in the only five houses on their block. Each house is a different color. Each friend has a different profession, and each owns a different pet. Use the clues to find the answer to this question: Who owns the aardvark?

Clues:

The musician lives in a yellow house.
The carpenter does not own an aardvark.
The inventor lives in the white house.
The yellow house is between the white and brown houses.
The hippo owner lives next door to the green house.
The musician does not live in the blue house.
The gecko lives next door to the python.
The python stays in the brown house.
The blue house is the last house.
The carpenter lives next door to the inventor.
The pastry chef does not keep piranhas.
The blue house is not home to the carpenter.
The carpenter has only one neighbor.
The optician lives between the musician and the pastry chef.
The musician has a fear of reptiles.
The chef does not own the aardvark.

Hint: page 64
Answer: page 59

Draw the pets in the correct houses.
Color each house with the correct color.
Write the profession of each owner under his/her house.

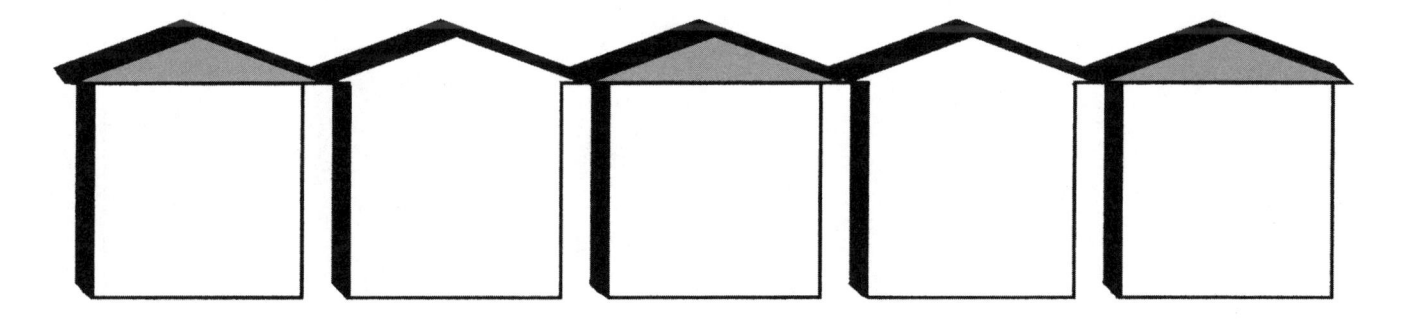

Puzzle 41: THE ANT AND THE HONEY

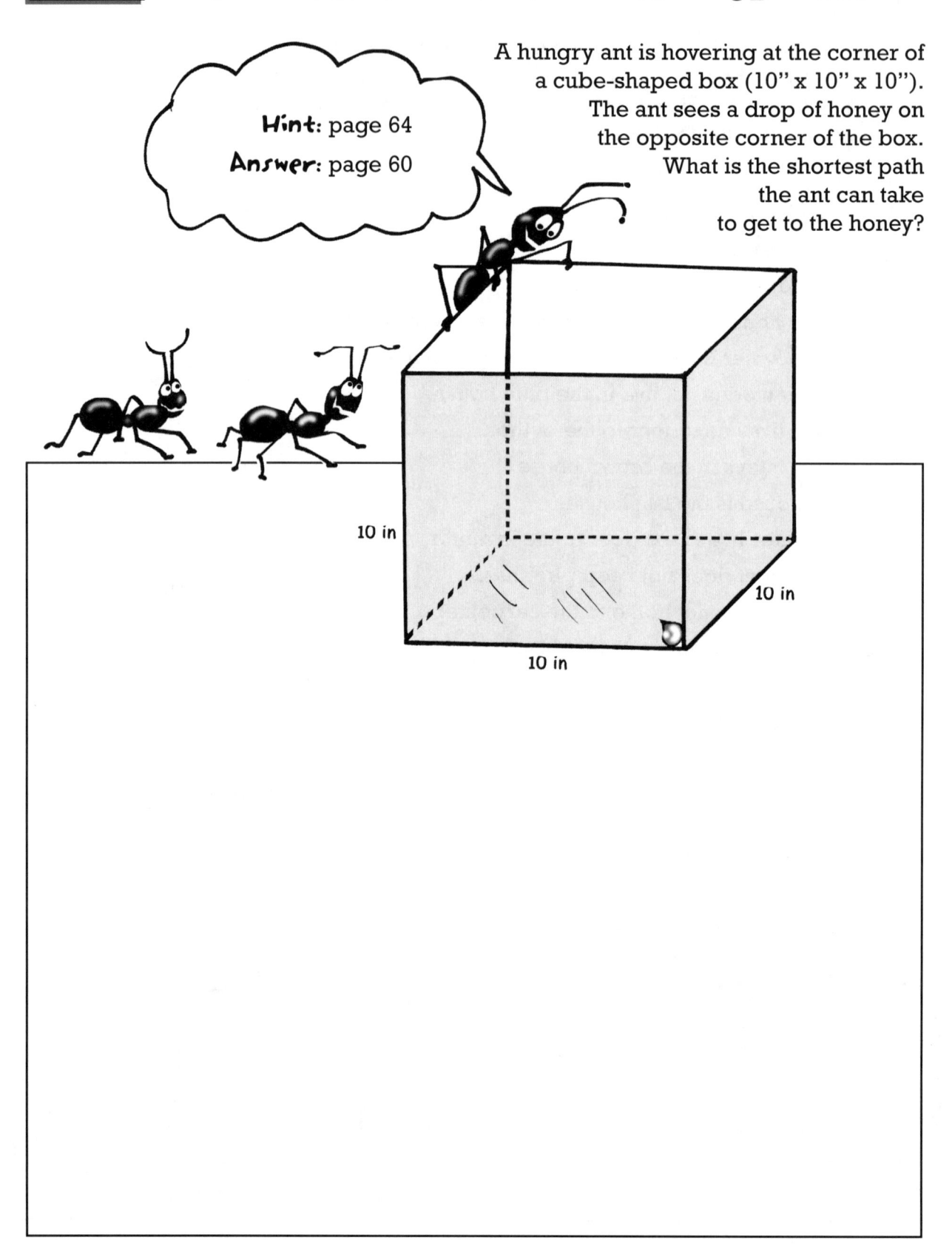

A hungry ant is hovering at the corner of a cube-shaped box (10" x 10" x 10"). The ant sees a drop of honey on the opposite corner of the box. What is the shortest path the ant can take to get to the honey?

Hint: page 64
Answer: page 60

10 in
10 in
10 in

Puzzle 42
How Wide Is The River?

Leonardo is preparing to build a bridge across a particular point in a river. Right now, he is standing on the bank of the river, and would like to measure its width. He has a measuring tape, but no way of crossing the river or throwing one end of the tape to the other side. What should he do to find the width of the river?

Hint: page 64
Answer: page 60

If it were up to me, I'd take a boat.

Very Challenging

Puzzle 43 — An Oily Predicament

The region of Chianti (Italy) is famous for its olive oil. One day, two brothers were sent to get oil from a shop. Each of them needed to buy two liters of oil. Dominic had an empty 4-liter container, and Anthony had an empty 5-liter container. When they got to the shop, the owner said, "Sorry, boys. I would like to help you, but I don't have a way to measure two liters. I have only these two 10-liter containers full of oil. I don't see how I can measure two liters for each of you." The boys thought for a while and came up with a solution. Can you figure out a solution?

(No other containers, empty or full, were available. There were no markings of any kind on any of the containers.)

Hint: page 64
Answer: page 60

Better hurry, Dom. Zia Sophia is waiting to cook pasta fazul.

Puzzle 44: A Hair-Splitting Query

Lucy asked her older brother if he thought that there were any two people in the world with exactly the same number of hairs on their heads. The brother answered, "How would I know? The only way to figure that out is to start counting people's hairs, and that would take forever..."

Lucy couldn't get this question out of her mind. She thought and thought, then went to get some information on the Internet. After just a few minutes, Lucy said to her brother, "I have an answer to my question. I'm sure there are at least two people in the world with the same number of hairs!" Her surprised brother asked: "Did they give you that information on the Internet?" Lucy replied, "No."

How, then, did she figure it out?

Hint: page 64
Answer: page 61

Puzzle 45: Friends + Acquaintances

Hundreds of people showed up at the most recent Star Trek convention. Jacob, one of the participants, said to Sam (another participant), "We Star Trek fans are such a unified group. In any group of four people you choose at random from this convention, there is at least one who knows all the other three."

I know you!

I was here last year, too.

"In that case," said Sam, "there must be at least one person here who knows everybody else at the convention."

Is this true?
If so, explain why.
Remember: Acquaintances are symmetric—if Jack knows Jill, then Jill knows Jack.

Hint: page 64
Answer: page 61

Very Challenging

Name_____

Puzzle It! Logic Puzzles and Tricks

Puzzle 46: Hats Off to the Guests!

Twenty clowns were invited to a party. After dinner, the host suggested the following game: The guests will be blindfolded, and the host will place a hat, either black or white, on the head of each guest. The guests will be ordered in a line, all facing the same direction, and the blindfolds will be removed. Thus, each guest will see the hats of everyone in front of him or her, but not the hat on his (or her) own head or on any of the guests behind.

Starting from the back of the line, each clown will guess the color of the hat on his or her head. While the clowns cannot see the hats of those behind them in line, they can hear all the guesses. For each correct guess, the group collectively receives $100 to be equally divided among all guests.

Before the game begins, the clowns can devise a strategy that will maximize their expected earnings.

Can you help them think of a strategy that will assure at least 19 correct guesses?

Hint: page 64
Answer: page 61

Very Challenging

Puzzle 47: The Mathematician's Wife

Dr. Cal Q. Layte (math professor) and his wife were invited to a party with four other couples. On the way over, the wife told the mathematician that he should try to be sociable at the party (instead of solving math problems in his head all the time as he usually did on such occasions).

In his attempt to make small talk, the mathematician asked all the other guests this question: "At this party, how many people have you greeted with a handshake?" He got nine different answers, from zero to eight.

At the end of the evening, Dr. Layte shared this finding with everybody in the party and asked, "Given only this information (nine different answers: zero to eight), can anyone determine how many people shook my wife's hand?"

What would be the correct answer? (Of course, no guest shook his or her own hand NOR the hand of his or her spouse.)

Hint: page 64

Answer: page 61

Very Challenging

Puzzle 48: The Democratic Pirates

A group of ten pirates found a treasure chest full of 100 gold coins. Each coin is VERY valuable. Although these pirates pride themselves on making decisions by voting, the structure of this group of pirates is quite hierarchical. Each pirate has an order of importance from one (the most important) to ten (the least important). They have a particular rule for making decisions such as dividing the treasure. Here's the way it works: Pirate Number One suggests a way to divide the treasure. The pirates vote on this suggestion. If 50 percent or more of the pirates (including Number One) are in favor, the treasure is divided according to the suggestion. If fewer than 50 percent are in favor, Pirate Number One gets thrown to the sharks. Then Pirate Number Two gets to suggest a method of dividing the gold, following the same rule ... and so on.

Imagine that you are Pirate Number One. What suggestion can you make that will guarantee your survival and make you rich?

Ahoy, Mateys!

There's gold enough for all!

Here's my plan...

Hint: page 64
Answer: page 62

Puzzle 49
Pasha's Problem

Pasha is creating a mosaic pattern around the pillar in a courtyard. She began by dividing the space into 1-foot squares. She established the following guidelines for her mosaic:

- The mosaic must have four congruent (the exact same shape and size) sections.
- The mosaic includes 24 special tiles (8 each of 3 different kinds).
- Each section must have the same number of each kind of special tile.

Pasha had pasted the special tiles in place, then lost her pattern.

Finish the mosaic by coloring in the four congruent sections. Remember, each section must include the same number of special tiles. The center square represents the pillar and may not be part of any section.

Hint: page 64
Answer: page 62

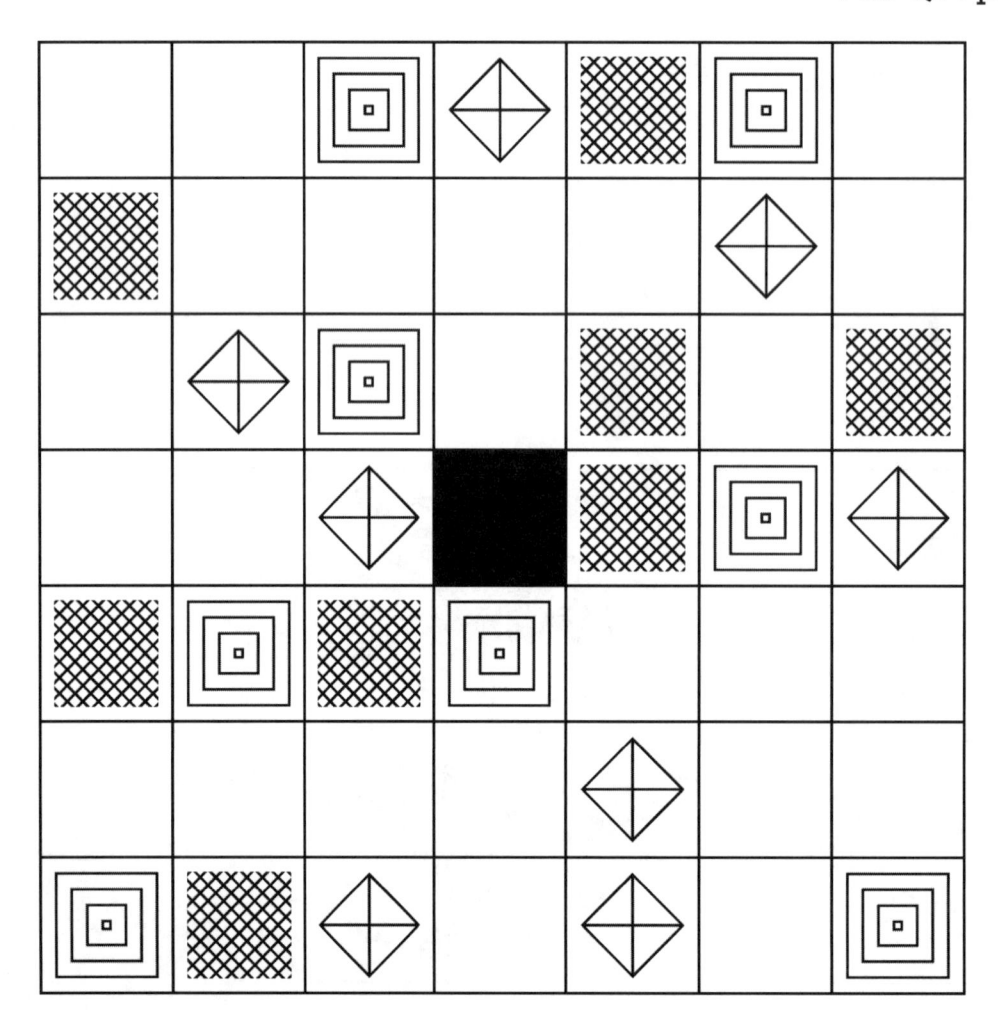

Name_____

Puzzle It! Logic Puzzles and Tricks   50   ©2007 by Incentive Publications, Inc., Nashville, TN.

Puzzle 50

A COLORFUL MESS

Clumsy Painter Pete was carrying two buckets of paint, one green and one red. He tripped and spilled the entire contents of both buckets, creating a colorful mess on the garage floor. The mess was more than a yard long and more than a yard wide. The colors did not blend, but swirled together into a pattern. Pete had a yardstick among his supplies. Prove that, no matter how complex the color pattern, Pete could always place the yardstick on the floor so that both ends would be on the same color.

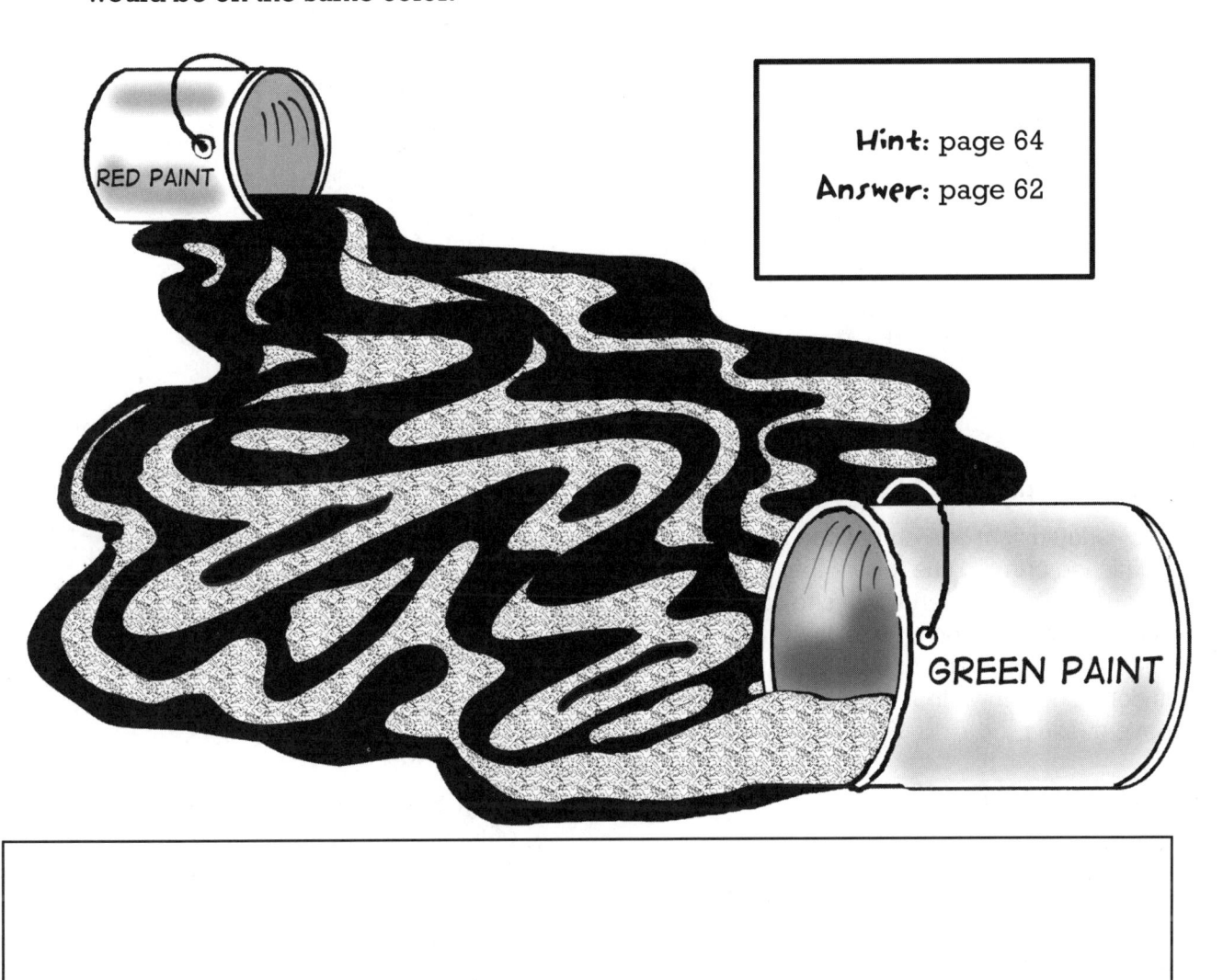

Hint: page 64
Answer: page 62

Very Challenging

ANSWER KEY

Puzzle 1 (pg 7)

Mix + Match

Form a pyramid with the matches!

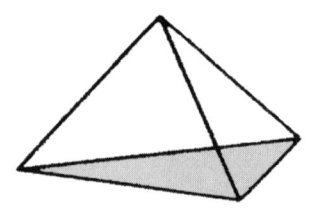

Puzzle 2 (pg 7)

Sock It to Me

Max will need to take three socks. He might be lucky and get a pair with the first two choices, but he can't be sure this will happen; the first two socks could be one white and one black. However, the third sock he selects is sure to complete one pair.

Puzzle 3 (pg 8)

Don't Miss the Boat

Lucy should light one end of one rope. When it is finished burning she knows that exactly 1 hour has passed, and then she can light the second rope from both ends. It will take the second rope half an hour to burn, and when it is done she knows that exactly 1 1/2 hours have passed.

Puzzle 4 (pg 9)

Relatively Puzzling

Todd, Rob, and their sister Alice are triplets.

Puzzle 5 (pg 9)

A Watery Dilemma

Here's what Nurse Terry can do:

Fill the 9-quart container. Pour water from it into the 4-quart container until that container is full. Empty the 4-quart container (not into the cooler), and again fill the 4-quart container with water from the 9-quart container. Now, there is 1 quart left in the 9-quart container.

Empty the 4-quart container, and pour the remaining 1 quart from the 9-quart container into the 4-quart container. Fill the 9-quart container again. Now, pour water from it into the 4-quart container (containing 1 quart) until it is full.

As exactly 3 quarts have been poured, the water remaining in the 9-quart container will measure exactly 6 quarts.

Puzzle 6 (pg 10)

Let Them Eat Cake

The cake should be cut from the top into four sections of the exact same size. Then the height of the cake should be sliced in half.

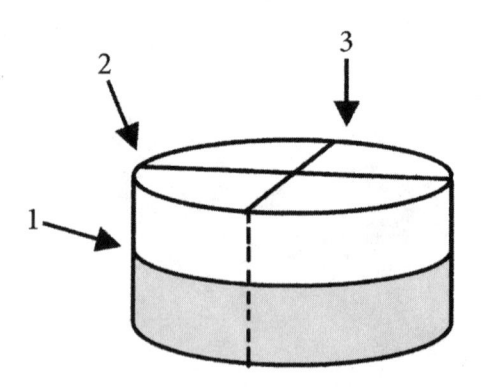

Puzzle 7 (pg 11)

To Tell the Truth

Each of the sentences is in contradiction to the other sixteen sentences. Thus, it is not possible that two (or more) sentences are true.

This leaves two possibilities:
Either all sentences are false, or there is one true statement.

All sentences cannot be false, because this would make sentence 17 true—in contradiction to the statement that all sentences are false.

All this means that there is exactly one sentence that is true, i.e. sixteen sentences that are false, and the true sentence must therefore be sentence 16.

Puzzle 8 (pg 12)
Liars + Truth-tellers

Commander DerLustt can ask the following question: "Do you live in this settlement?"

If the answer is "yes", there are two possibilities:

1. The alien is a truth-teller, and astronaut Juan is in the truth-tellers' settlement.
2. The alien is a liar, which means that the reply is a lie and she really lives in the other settlement, which again means that Juan is in the truth-tellers' settlement.

If the answer is "no", again there are two possibilities:

1. The alien is a truth-teller, and Juan is in the liars' settlement.
2. The alien is a liar. Therefore, her/his reply is a lie and she does live in this settlement. Thus, Juan is in the liars' settlement.

So . . . if the answer is "yes" he is in the truth-tellers' settlement, and if the answer is "no" he is in the liars' settlement—regardless of the home-settlement of the inhabitant who gives the answer.

Puzzle 9 (pg 13)
Conundrum on the Ice

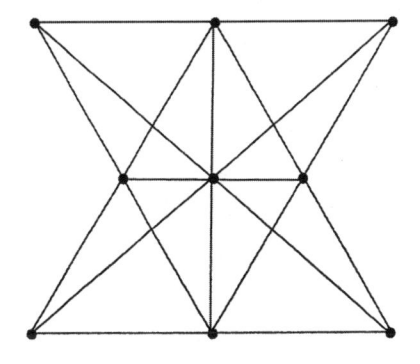

Puzzle 10 (pg 14)
Talking Turtles

The first or third turtle is walking backwards.

Puzzle 11 (pg 15)
Pirate Jack's Dilemma

Jack can put the treasure in the trunk, lock the trunk with his lock, and ship it to Fran. She can put her lock on the trunk and ship it back (with both locks on). When Jack gets the trunk, he can take his lock off and send it back with Fran's lock on. Fran will get the trunk, open her lock with her key and put the treasure somewhere else for safekeeping.

Puzzle 12 (pg 16)
The Queen's Necklace

All four links of one of the short chains can be opened and closed as shown below, costing only $40.

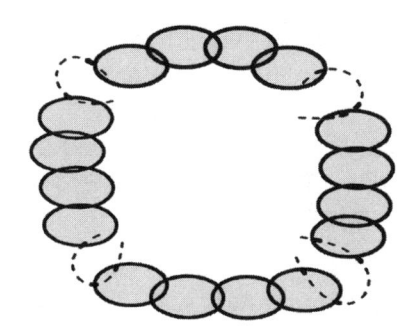

Puzzle 13 (pg 17)
Who Found the Mermaid?

Harry photographed the mermaid in Australia.
Larry photographed a lobster in Hawaii.
Terry photographed a sunken ship in Bermuda.
Mary photographed a treasure chest in Belize.

	LOCATION			
	Hawaii	Belize	Bermuda	Australia
Mary	X	O	X	X
Larry	O	(X)	(X)	(X)
Harry	X	X	(X)	O
Terry	X	(X)	O	X

	FAVORITE PHOTO			
	Sunken Ship	Treasure Chest	Lobster	Mermaid
Mary	X	O	X	X
Larry	O	(X)	O	X
Harry	(X)	X	X	✻
Terry	O	X	X	X

Puzzle 14 (pg 18)

Are You in Accord?

The clownfish is the mascot for the first floor.

Remember, each attribute is associated with only one floor, so once the location of an attribute has been identified, it is excluded from being the attribute (in that category) for any other floor.

Read the hints carefully and record any information that is known. It is helpful to construct a series of charts or grids, as shown below, to keep track of facts as they are discovered. Then reread the hints and continue to build on the information you collect, unraveling the mystery until you solve the puzzle.
(Hint: Mark through statements that you have already used to help keep track of statements that you still need to apply.)

At the first read-through, you know that the first floor holds discussion meetings on Thursday and the third floor serves pizza rolls at their discussion meetings.

Meeting Day

	Mon	Tue	Wed	Thu	Fri
5				x	
4				x	
3				x	
2				x	
1	x	x	x	O	x

Snacks

	Twinkies	chips	pizza	fruit	cookies
5			x		
4			x		
3	x	x	O	x	x
2			x		
1			x		

SUMMARY

FLOOR	Elevator Door	Common Interest	Mascot	Snack	Meeting Day
5					
4					
3				pizza rolls	
2					
1					Thurs

At the second read-through, you discover that the third floor has a white elevator door (because these people have pizza sauce on their fingers since they have pizza rolls for snacks), and the second floor has a blue elevator door (because the blue door is next to the floor with Thursday meetings, and there is no floor beneath the floor with Thursday meetings).

Elevator Door

	red	yellow	green	white	blue
5				x	x
4				x	x
3	x	x	x	O	x
2	x	x	x	x	O
1				x	x

SUMMARY

FLOOR	Elevator Door	Common Interest	Mascot	Snack	Meeting Day
5					
4					
3	white			pizza rolls	
2	blue				
1					Thurs

At the third read-through, you find that the fourth floor has a green elevator door (because it is on the floor above the white door), and also that these are the ones who serve chips as a snack.

Elevator Door

	red	yellow	green	white	blue
5			x	x	x
4	x	x	O	x	x
3	x	x	x	O	x
2	x	x	x	x	O
1			x	x	x

Snacks

	Twnk.	chips	pizza	fruit	cook.
5		x	x		
4	x	O	x	x	x
3	x	x	O	x	x
2		x	x		
1		x	x		

SUMMARY

FLOOR	Elevator Door	Common Interest	Mascot	Snack	Meeting Day
5					
4	green			chips	
3	white			pizza rolls	
2	blue				
1					Thurs

Continue in this manner until all cells except one are filled in; the blank cell is the answer. Completed grids are shown below.

Elevator Door

	red	yellow	green	white	blue
5	O	x	x	x	x
4	x	x	O	x	x
3	x	x	x	O	x
2	x	x	x	x	O
1	x	O	x	x	x

Snacks

	Twnk.	chips	pizza	fruit	cook.
5	x	x	x	x	O
4	x	O	x	x	x
3	x	x	O	x	x
2	O	x	x	x	x
1	x	x	x	O	x

Puzzle It! Logic Puzzles and Tricks

Common Interest

	books	cars	fitness	current events	antiques
5	O	x	x	x	x
4	x	x	O	x	x
3	x	x	x	x	O
2	x	x	x	O	x
1	x	O	x	x	x

Meeting Day

	Mon	Tue	Wed	Thu	Fri
5	O	x	x	x	x
4	x	O	x	x	x
3	x	x	x	x	O
2	x	x	O	x	x
1	x	x	x	O	x

Mascot

	fish	pug	owl	cat	pig
5	x	x	O	x	x
4	x	O	x	x	x
3	x	x	x	O	x
2	x	x	x	x	O
1	O	x	x	x	x

SUMMARY

FLOOR	Elevator Door	Common Interest	Mascot	Snack	Meeting Day
5	red	books	owl	cookies	Mon
4	green	physical fitness	pug	chips	Tue
3	white	antiques	cat	pizza rolls	Fri
2	blue	current events	pig	Twinkies	Wed
1	yellow	fast cars		fruit	Thurs

Puzzle 15 (pg 19)

An Anniversary Toast

Step	Action	Status 8 oz	Status 5 oz	Status 3 oz
0		8	0	0
1	Fill 3-oz glass from the 8-oz container	5	0	3
2	Pour 3 oz into 5-oz glass	5	3	0
3	Fill 3-oz glass again	2	3	3
4	Fill 5-oz glass with juice from 3-oz glass	2	5	1
5	Pour all the juice from the 5-oz glass into the 8-oz container	7	0	1
6	Move the 1 oz left in the 3-oz glass to the 5-oz glass	7	1	0
7	Fill the 3-oz glass from the 8-oz glass	4	1	3
8	Pour the juice from the 3-oz glass into the 5-oz glass	4	4	0

Puzzle 16 (pg 20)

Fire on the Island

The shepherd can take the sheep toward the center of the island. Then, he can use the fire to light a dry branch and set a new fire near the south end of the island. The fire he sets will spread southward, stopping at the end of the island, creating an area that is burned. Then he can take the sheep southward to this burned area. When the (original) fire approaches, they (and he) will be protected, because the fire will have nothing to burn in this area.

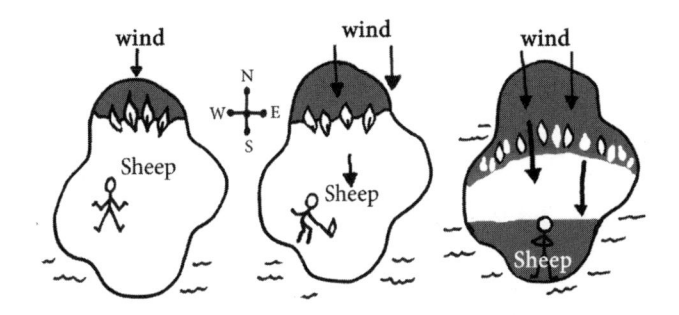

Puzzle 17 (pg 21)

A Ringing Question

When the bell rings six times, there are five time intervals between the rings. Thus, the time between rings is $\frac{6}{5}$ seconds. When the bell rings 11 times, there are 10 time intervals. Therefore, it takes $10 \times \frac{6}{5}$, or 12 seconds.

Puzzle 18 (pg 21)

The Confused Professor

If nine of the letters are in the right envelopes, the tenth letter must also be in the right envelope. Thus, it is impossible to get exactly nine letters right. (In other words, the chance is zero!)

Puzzle 19 (pg 22)

Counterfeit Coins

He can put this combination on the scales: One coin from the first bag, two coins from the second bag, three coins from the third, etc.

Thus, there are 36 coins on the scales $(1 + 2 + 3 + \ldots + 8 = 36)$. If all coins were gold they would have weighed 360 grams. However, the news report let him know that some of the coins are counterfeit.

(continued)

If the 36 coins weigh 359 grams, this means that only one coin on the scales is counterfeit, and therefore the first bag contains the counterfeit coins.

Similarly, if the coins weigh 358 grams, this means that two coins are counterfeit, and that the second bag contains the bad coins, and so on.

Puzzle 20 (pg 23)

Don't Lift That Pen!

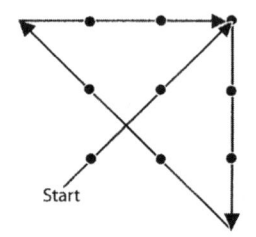

Puzzle 21 (pg 24)

Tricky Timekeeping!

She can turn both hourglasses simultaneously. When the sand in the 4-minute hourglass has finished pouring, she should stop the 7-minute hourglass by laying it down horizontally.

She now has 3 minutes' worth of sand in one side of the 7-minute hourglass, and 4 minutes' worth of sand on the other. Again, she should simultaneously turn both hourglasses, with sand flowing from the side of the 7-minute hourglass containing 3 minutes' worth of sand. When the sand in the 7-minute hourglass has finished pouring, she can stop the 4-minute hourglass, which will have 1 minute's worth left on one side.

Then she should turn both hourglasses, with sand pouring from the side with 1 minute's worth of the 4-minute hourglass. When this sand has finished pouring, she should stop the 7-minute hourglass, which will now have 1 minute's worth on one side.

At this stage she is ready to measure 9 minutes by doing this: Turn only the 4-minute hourglass. When the sand has all poured, reverse the 4-minute hourglass. When the sand has again all poured, 8 minutes will have passed.

Now, turn the 7-minute hourglass with sand flowing from the side with 1 minute's worth. When it has finished, exactly 9 (4 + 4 + 1) minutes have passed.

Puzzle 22 (pg 24)

Another Timely Trick

Bee can simultaneously turn both hourglasses. When the sand in the 7-minute hourglass has finished pouring, she should stop the 11-minute hourglass by laying it down horizontally. She now will have 7 minutes' worth of sand in one side of the 11-minute hourglass, and 4 minutes' worth of sand on the other. This stage is described as "stage 1" in the table below. She can follow the stages in the table, until she has 10 minutes' worth of sand on one side of the 11-minute hourglass.

The verbal description of these stages is: Simultaneously turn the 7-minute hourglass and the 11-minute hourglass, with sand pouring from the side with 4 minutes' worth. When the sand in the 11-minute hourglass has finished pouring, 4 minutes have passed. Stop the 7-minute hourglass, which now has 4 minutes' worth of sand on one side, and 3 minutes worth on the other. Turn both hourglasses, with sand pouring out of the 3-minute side in the 7-minute hourglass. When this stage is done you will have 3 minutes' worth on one side of the 11-minute hourglass, and 8 minutes' worth on the other. Next, turn both hourglasses, with sand pouring out of the 8-minute side in the 11-minute hourglass. When the sand has finished pouring in the 7-minute hourglass, stop, and now you have 1 minute's worth on one side of the 11-minute hourglass, and 10 minutes' worth on the other.

At this stage you are ready to measure 17 minutes. Turn only the 11-minute hourglass with sand pouring from the 10-minute side. When the sand has all poured, turn the 7-minute hourglass. When it has finished, 17 (10 + 7) minutes have passed.

Stage	11-minute hourglass		7-minute hourglass	
	Sand on side A	Sand on side B	Sand on side A	Sand on side B
0	11	0	7	0
1	4	7	0	7
2	0	11	4	3
3	3	8	7	0
4	10	1	0	7
Ready to measure!				

Puzzle 23 (pg 25)

Troublesome Ladies

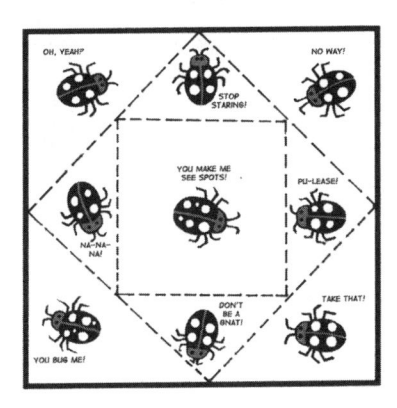

Puzzle 24 (pg 26)

A Wise Gardener

Draw five lines any way you want, making sure that no two lines are parallel. Each line must touch each of the other four lines, and each pair of lines crosses at a different point (see illustration below).

Plant the trees at the intersection points. Every line will have four intersection points (with the other four lines), and thus will have four trees planted on it. The total number of trees planted will be ten.

Puzzle 25 (pg 27)

A Puzzling Match-up

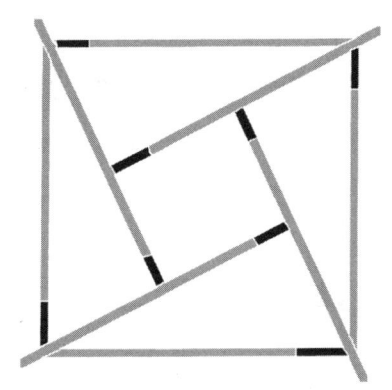

Puzzle 26 (pg 27)

To Be or Knot To Be

Fold your arms across your chest naturally. Make sure your right hand is resting on the bend of your left elbow. Reach over the top of the left elbow with your right hand and pick up the left end of the string.

Now tuck your left hand down under your right elbow. Reach that left hand out to pick up the right-hand end of the string. Pull both your hands in toward the center of your body.

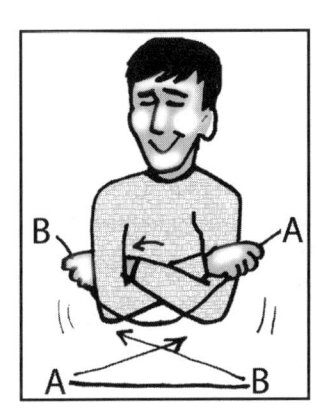

The string will be wrapped around your left arm. Carefully slide your arm out of the string, and as you untie your hands, the string will form a knot!

Puzzle 27 (pg 28)

Coffee with Milk, Please!

At the end of the process the amount of liquid in each of the containers is exactly what it was before she started (because she took one cup and poured one cup into each of the containers). Therefore, the amount of coffee "missing" from the coffee container (the coffee that is now in the milk container) is exactly equal to the amount of milk added to the coffee container. In other words, there is exactly the same amount of coffee in the milk container as there is milk in the coffee container.

Puzzle 28 (pg 29)

A Fork in the Road

Alexander can ask the resident the following question: "If I were to point at this road and ask you: 'Is this the right way?' would you answer 'Yes'?"

If the resident is a truth-teller and Alexander is pointing in the right direction, the resident will answer "Yes." If Alexander is pointing the wrong way, the resident will answer "No."

If the resident is a liar, and Alexander is pointing the right way, the native would answer "No" to the direct question, "Is this the right way?" So when asked, "Would you answer 'Yes' if this is the right way?" the true answer is "No". But as this person is a liar, the answer would be "yes." If Alexander is pointing the wrong way, the liar would answer "No".

In short, Alexander will get the same answers from both the liar and the truth-teller: If the answer is "Yes", this means that Alexander is pointing the right direction. If the answer is "No", he is pointing the wrong way.

Puzzle 29 (pg 30)

The King's Gifts

The king opens the crate with the sign "Gold + Silver" and takes out one coin. As all signs are incorrect, this crate truly cannot be the mixed crate.

Therefore, if the coin is golden, the opened crate is the one with golden coins. In this case, the crate with the sign "Silver" is the one with mixed coins, and the crate with the sign "Gold + Silver" contains the silver coins.

If the coin taken out is silver, this means that the opened crate is the one with silver coins, the crate with the sign "Silver" contains the golden coins, and the one with the sign "Gold" contains the mixed coins.

Puzzle 30 (pg 31)

The Great Egg-Drop

Only one egg has to be smashed! The scientist starts by dropping the egg from the first floor. If the eggshell doesn't smash, he takes the same egg and drops it from the second floor, and so on. This is repeated until the scientist finds the first floor from which the eggshell smashes.

Puzzle 31 (pg 32)

Wonderful Wands

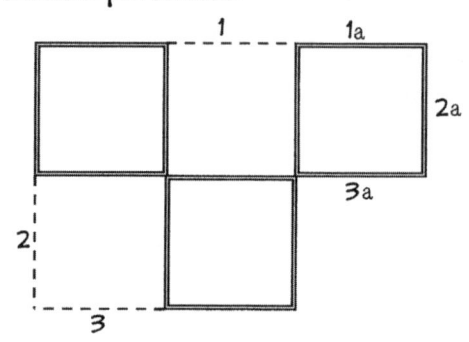

Puzzle 32 (pg 33)

Some Fortress!

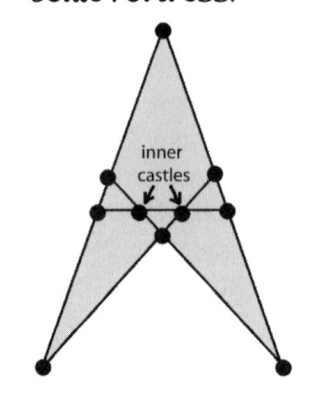

Puzzle 33 (pg 34)

A Chocolate-y Quandary

The first two sisters each get 2 full barrels, 2 empty barrels, and 3 barrels that are half full. The third sister gets the barrels that are left: 3 full barrels, 3 empty barrels, and one half-full barrel. Thus, each sister gets 3.5 barrels of syrup.

Puzzle 34 (pg 35)

Sixteen Points

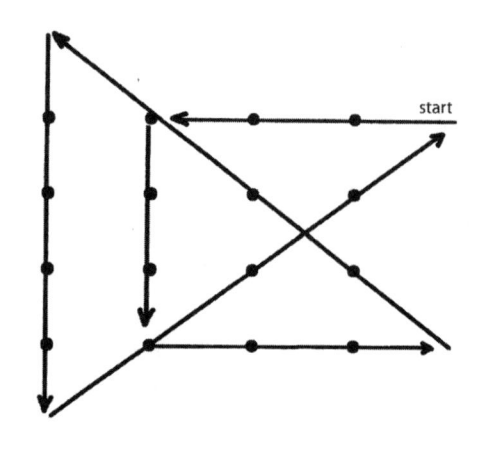

Puzzle It! Logic Puzzles and Tricks ©2007 by Incentive Publications, Inc., Nashville, TN.

Puzzle 35 (pg 36)
Positioning the Pillars

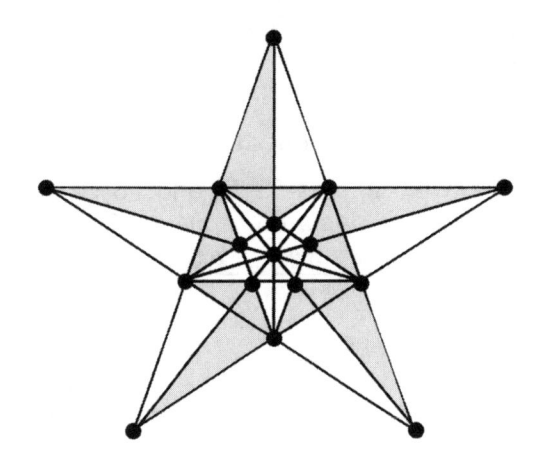

Puzzle 36 (pg 37)
Family Crossings

The two children cross. One child remains on the other side, and the other child returns with the boat. Now, one of the parents crosses, and the child that remained on the other side returns with the boat.

Repeat the whole sequence beginning with the two children crossing. After the second parent crosses, the child on one side must go back across and finally, the two children cross together.

Puzzle 37 (pg 38)
Draw the Envelope

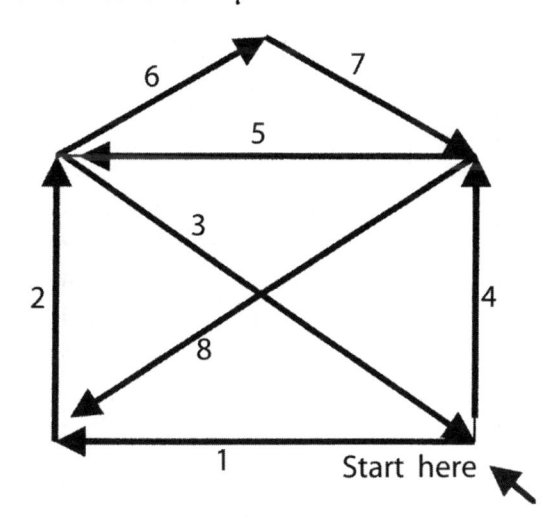

This is one solution; there are many.

Puzzle 38 (pg 39)
The Sugar in the Goblet

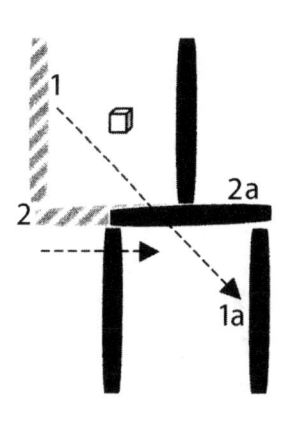

Puzzle 39 (pg 40)
Pet Crossings

Agatha takes the cat across. Then she returns, gets the dog and takes the dog back across.

When she gets to the other side she leaves the dog and takes the cat back.

She leaves the cat (on the original side of the bridge) and takes the mouse over to the dog.

Finally, she returns, gets the cat and takes it back to the other side.

Puzzle 40 (pg 41)
Who Owns the Aardvark?

The musician.

First house—green, carpenter, piranhas

Second house—white, inventor, hippo

Third house—yellow, musician, aardvark

Fourth house—brown, optician, python

Fifth house—blue, pastry chef, gecko

Puzzle 41 (pg 42)

The Ant and the Honey

The best way to see the shortest path is to imagine "opening" the box (see diagram). The shortest connection between two points is a straight line, and that is the path the ant should take (the line AH in the figure).

Going straight down to the floor and then crossing it diagonally (dashed line) is a longer path.

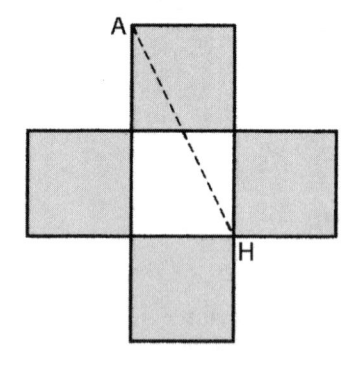

Puzzle 42 (pg 43)

How Wide Is the River?

Leonardo should find a noticeable object on the other side of the river (such as the tree in the figure below) and give this point a name (such as T). Then he should stand on his bank of the river exactly across from that object and place a stick in the ground there (point S_1).

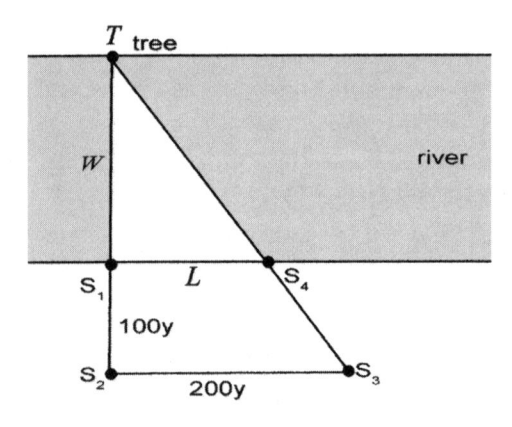

Next, he should walk 100 yards away from the river to point S_2 (keeping the tree, his stick at S_1, and himself aligned) and place a stick at S_2. Then, he should walk 200 yards parallel to the river (to point S_3 in the figure) and also mark this point with a stick.

Standing at S_3, he should look at the tree, and note the spot on his bank of the river (point S_4) that is directly in his line of sight as he looks at the tree. He should walk to this point (S_4), measure the distance from it to the stick at S_1, and name this distance L.

Now he can figure out the width of the river, w:

As the two triangles TS_1S_4 and TS_2S_3 are similar, their sides are proportional, i.e:

$$\frac{W + 100}{W} = \frac{200}{L}$$

This can be written as:

$$\frac{100}{W} = \frac{200}{L} - 1 \quad \text{or} \quad \frac{1}{W} = \frac{\frac{200}{L} - 1}{100}$$

$$\text{or} \quad W = \frac{100}{\frac{200}{L} - 1}$$

Thus, once he has measured L, he can figure out W. For example, if L is 40 yards, he will know that the river is 25 yards wide. (The distances of 100 yards and 200 yards chosen here are arbitrary, and the solution works with any other distances as well.) If the distances are d_1 and d_2, respectively, the general formula for the width is:

$$W = \frac{d_1}{\frac{d_2}{L} - 1}$$

Puzzle 43 (pg 44)

An Oily Dilemma

The boys' plan is given in the table below, indicating the amount of oil in each container at each stage:

stage	4-liter cont	5-liter cont	10-liter cont	10-liter cont
initial	0	0	10	10
1	0	5	5	10
2	4	1	5	10
3	0	1	9	10
4	1	0	9	10
5	1	5	4	10
6	4	5	4	7
7	0	5	8	7
8	0	2	8	10
9	4	2	8	6
final	2	2	10	6

Can you think of a solution with fewer stages?

Puzzle 44 (pg 45)

A Hair-splitting Query

The average number of hairs per person is about 150,000. The number of people on the planet is about 6,400,000,000. Suppose that every person had a different number of hairs. In that case, we could arrange everybody in an order from the person with the least hair (0) to the one with the most. Person number 2 in the order would have at least 1 hair (he could have more, but no less, because person number 1 on the list has 0 hairs). Similarly, person number 1,000 on the list would have at least 999 hairs.

In the same way, the last person on the list would at least 6,399,999,999 hairs. As there is no person with so many hairs (or even remotely close, since the average number of hairs per person is about 150,000), we must conclude that there are some people with the same number of hairs.

Put differently, if no two people had the same number of hairs, the average number of hairs would to be (at least) 3,200,000,000 (6,400,000,000 ÷ 2), much, much more than the actual average number of 150,000.

Puzzle 45 (pg 46)

Friends + Acquaintances

Suppose that there was not a single person who knew everybody else. This means that for every person there is at least one person in the convention that he doesn't know. If this is true then there would have to be groups of four people where none of the four knows all the other three, in contradiction to the first statement in the puzzle. Therefore, if the first statement is true (in every group of four there is one who knows all the other three), there must be one person (at least) who knows everybody else.

Consider any person (designated A). Assume there is at least one person that A doesn't know. (For the purpose of proving the argument, we are assuming that nobody knows everybody else.) Call this second person B. Now, there must be a third person who knows both A and B. (Otherwise, it would mean that any person in the convention either does not know A, or does not know B. In that case, in the foursome A + B + any other two people, there is nobody who knows all the other three, in contradiction to the first statement.) Let's call this third person (who knows both A and B) C. There must be someone whom C doesn't know (by our assumption), whom we can call D.

Now, in the group of A, B, C, and D, there is no one who knows the other three: A doesn't know B, B doesn't know A, C doesn't know D, and D doesn't know C. This contradicts the first statement which asserts that in every group of four there is one who knows all the other three. Therefore, if the first statement is true, there must be at least one person who knows everybody else.

Puzzle 46 (pg 47)

Hats Off to the Guests!

The following strategy assures at least 19 correct guesses: The first person to guess, the one who is last in line, looks at the hats in front of him. If he sees an even number of black hats he says "black" and if he sees an odd number of black hats he says "white". Of course, what he says does not necessarily match the color of his own hat, and his guess may be incorrect.

Now, the second person to guess, the one before last in line, looks at the number of black hats in front of him. From this number, and what the first person said, he can find out the color of his own hat. For example, if the first person said "black" indicating that he saw an even number of black hats, and the second person also sees an even number of black hats, this means that the second person's hat must be white.

If the first person said "black" and the second person sees an odd number of black hats, this means that the second person's hat is black.

Similarly, if the first person said "white" and the second person sees an even number of black hats, the second person's hat must be black. Thus, the second person can deduce the color of his hat, and his guess will be correct.

(continued)

The third person knows three things:

1) the reply of the first person
2) the color of the second person's hat (which he knows from the second person's reply), and
3) the number of black hats in front of him.

From these three things he can deduce the color of his hat. For example, if the first person saw an even number of black hats, the second person's hat is white, and the third person sees an odd number of black hats, this must mean that the color of the third person's hat must be black, and so forth.

So the third person can also correctly deduce the color of his hat. Similarly, every person in line can correctly deduce the color of his hat from the reply of the first person, the guesses of everybody before him, and the number of black hats he sees in front of him.

Puzzle 47 (pg 48)

The Mathematician's Wife

Let us refer to the guests by the number of hands they shook; for example, "8" is the guest who shook the hands of 8 people. We don't know how many hands the mathematician shook, so let's refer to him as M.

Guest 8 shook the hands of eight people, so these must be 1, 2, 3, 4, 5, 6, 7, and M. (Guest 8 did not shake the hand of 0, because 0 shook hands with nobody.) On the other hand, the only two people in the party that 8 did not shake hands with are himself or herself and his or her spouse. So 8's spouse must be 0.

Guest 7 shook the hands of 7 people. These must be 2, 3, 4, 5, 6, 8, and M. How do we know that 7 did not shake the hand of 1? Because 1 shook only one hand, and we know that he or she shook the hand of 8. Thus, 7 shook the hands of everybody except 0, 1, and himself or herself. As 0 is the spouse of 8, 7's spouse must be 1. Similarly, the spouse of 6 is 2, and the spouse of 5 is 3. The spouse of M is therefore 4, i.e., the mathematician's wife shook the hands of four people.

Puzzle 48 (pg 49)

The Democratic Pirates

Suppose that only Pirates 9 and 10 had been left. In this case, Pirate 9 would suggest 100 coins for himself and 0 for Pirate 10. Pirate 10 would vote against, but the offer would be approved because Pirate 9 would vote for, and 50 percent of the votes is enough.

Now, suppose that only Pirates 8, 9, and 10 were left. What would 8 suggest? He knows that he needs two votes. One of these is his own vote, so he needs either 9 or 10 to vote for his suggestion. Whom would it be easier to convince? Pirate 9 only loses if 8's offer is approved, because if it is rejected he will be left with 10, and will get all 100 coins for himself. However, 10 can only gain if 8's offer is approved (because otherwise he gets nothing). So 8 will offer 1 coin to 10, nothing to 9, and 99 coins to himself.

Suppose now that Pirates 7, 8, 9, and 10 are left. What would 7 suggest? 7 needs two votes, himself and somebody else. Who would be cheapest to "buy"? It would be Pirate 9, who gets nothing if 7's offer is rejected and 8 makes the offer. So 7 suggests 1 coin for 9, nothing for 8 and 10, and 99 coins for himself (see table below).

If 6, 7, 8, 9, and 10 are left, 6 needs three votes. He will therefore offer 8 and 10 (who get nothing if 7 makes the offer) one coin, and 98 coins for himself.

Continuing this logic, the offer that Pirate 1 makes, and which is accepted, is this: 96 coins for Pirate 1, one coin to Pirates 9, 7, 5, 3, and nothing for the rest. (So much for democracy!)

Thus, nobody gets fed to the sharks.

Pirate	10	9	8	7	6	5	4	3	2	1
The offer of pirate 9:	0	100								
The offer of pirate 8:	1	0	99							
The offer of pirate 7:	0	1	0	99						
The offer of pirate 6:	1	0	1	0	98					
The offer of pirate 5:	0	1	0	1	0	98				
The offer of pirate 4:	1	0	1	0	1	0	97			
The offer of pirate 3:	0	1	0	1	0	1	0	97		
The offer of pirate 2:	1	0	1	0	1	0	1	0	96	
The offer of pirate 1:	0	1	0	1	0	1	0	1	0	96

Puzzle 49 (pg 50)

Pasha's Problem

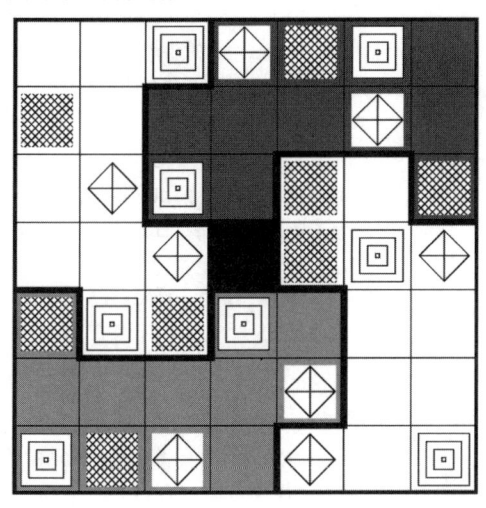

Puzzle 50 (pg 51)

A Colorful Mess

Imagine an equilateral triangle—with each side one yard long—lying on the floor. At least two of the corners of this triangle are on the same color (after all, each corner can be on only one of two colors). If you place the yardstick so that its ends are on these two spots, the two stick ends will both be on the same color.

HINTS FOR SOLVING PROBLEMS

Puzzle 1
Try to think "outside the box" of flat dimensions.

Puzzle 2
The answer does not change if you have 44 white socks and 117 black socks.

Puzzle 3
The ropes can be burned from either end?

Puzzle 4
Their sister is not much older than they are.

Puzzle 5
If you fill the 9-quart container and empty enough of it to fill the 4-quart container, you know that you will have exactly five quarts remaining in the 9-quart container.

Puzzle 6
Friends don't care how much frosting they get.

Puzzle 7
The first sentence can't be true because if there is only one false statement, this makes sentences 2 through 17 false (contradicting the statement in the first sentence).

Puzzle 8
Commander DerLusst does not know whether the alien is a liar or a truth-teller. He must ask a question to help him figure out which village he's in regardless of whether or not the alien answers truthfully.

Puzzle 9
In this example below, only eight lines are possible. However, if you move just two pucks, you can use ten lines!

Puzzle 10
These particular turtles are not capable of lying. So what's going on?

Puzzle 11
Jack doesn't mind shipping the treasure more than once, as long as it is locked up.

Puzzle 12
The goldsmith's solution will cost only $40.

Puzzle 13
Which locations are in the Pacific Ocean?

Puzzle 14
There are five floors and five different categories for each floor. Create a table and record what you know to determine where the fish belongs.

Puzzle 15
Start by filling the 3-ounce glass and pouring the three ounces into the 5-ounce glass. Then fill the 3-ounce glass again from the 8-ounce container.

Puzzle 16
A dry branch will be useful for the solution.

Puzzle 17
It takes more than eleven seconds.

Puzzle 18
No calculations are necessary.

Puzzle 19
The weighing involves coins from each of the eight bags.

Puzzle 20
Use out-of-the-box thinking. Don't be square.

Puzzle 21
Bee should start by preparing the 7-minute hourglass so it has one minute's worth of sand on one side.

Puzzle 22
Bee should begin by preparing the 11-minute hourglass so there are ten minutes worth of sand on one side and one minute on the other.

Puzzle 23
The square fences are not all the same size.

Puzzle 24
There are many different solutions. The designs that fulfill the requirements are not necessarily symmetrical.

Puzzle 25
The triangles are all the same size. The squares are not.

Puzzle 26
You don't have to hold the left end of the string with your left hand and the right end with your right hand.

Puzzle 27
The solution does not depend on the size of the containers or the size of the cup.

Puzzle 28
A direct question like, "Is this the right way?" won't help Alexander. He does not know if the person is a truth-teller or a liar. He should think of an indirect question.

Puzzle 29
Do not open the box labeled GOLD.

Puzzle 30
The eggs may or may not smash when dropped. They don't get weaker if they have been dropped before.

Puzzle 31
The three wands to be moved are not all from the same square.

Puzzle 32
The solution is not necessarily symmetrical.

Puzzle 33
Two of the sisters get the same combination of barrels, but the third gets a different combination.

Puzzle 34
Don't let edges or boundaries constrain you.

Puzzle 35
Not all the lines are of the same length. There are five long lines, five intermediate-length lines, and five short lines.

Puzzle 36
More than one family member will have to cross the river more than once.

Puzzle 37
There is definitely more than one solution.

Puzzle 38
The goblet can change positions.

Puzzle 39
The cat crosses the bridge more than once.

Puzzle 40
Piranhas are not kept next door to the python.

Puzzle 41
Going straight down the side and crossing the bottom diagonally is not the shortest path.

Puzzle 42
The solution requires some simple geometry. Refresh your memory about the concept of similar triangles. Two similar triangles have the same shape, they have the same angles, and the lengths of their sides are proportional.

Puzzle 43
Begin by figuring a way to get one of the 10-liter containers to hold exactly seven liters of oil.

Puzzle 44
From Internet sources, Lucy learned the average number of hairs a person has is about 150,000, and the number of people in the world is about 6.4 billion.

Puzzle 45
Prove that the opposite assumption—that there was no single person who knew everybody else—is false. Then Sam's statement must be true. This would mean that for each person attending, there is at least one other person at the convention he/she doesn't know.

Puzzle 46
The first guesser, at the back of the line, who can see all the hats except his/her own, may guess wrong. A good strategy can insure that all the other guesses are right.

Puzzle 47
One of the guests shook the hands of eight people. Figure out how many different hands that guest's spouse shook.

Puzzle 48
First Hint: Every pirate is greedy. Each will get as much as possible for himself, give away as little as possible to stay alive, and take any amount of gold, even if small. Each pirate is brilliant and skilled in logic.

Second Hint: Suppose that only Pirates 9 and 10 are left. What partition of the gold would Number 9 suggest? (Remember, 50% of the vote is enough to approve the offer.)

Puzzle 49
Each section of the mosaic represents a tessellation of a 3' x 4' rectangle.

Puzzle 50
Suppose Pete chose three different points in the color spill. Can each point be on a different color?